The Blessing Of Tough Experiences

Overcoming Challenging Situations
To Eventual Success

By

DR. EDDIE JERNAGIN

The Blessings Of Tough Experiences

(Overcoming Challenging Situations To Eventual Success)

Published By:

ABM Publications

A division of Andrew Bills Ministries Inc.
PO Box 6811
Orange, CA 92863

ISBN: 978-1-931820-11-0

Library of Congress Control Number

DEDICATION

This book is lovingly dedicated to my lovely wife,
Mamie Elizabeth Jernagin,
who has been my faithful companion
and my closest friend for many years.

TABLE OF CONTENTS

PREFACE

Life is an ongoing adventure of experiences composed of favorable situations, as well as those moments we would rather not have as a part of our personal experience. Tough times conquered however, have a way of ironically contributing to positive growth and development in our life in a way that non-challenging experiences can never do.

The wisdom of scripture reveals a profound truth the immature mind perhaps can never quite understand. It states that "...**all things work together for good to them that love God, to them who are the called according to his purpose.**" (Romans 8:28)

The profound truth stated in the preceding verse of scripture becomes personally realistic as God gives to those who seek His counsel victory after victory when they adhere in a disciplined manner to wise spiritual principles made available for those who permit biblical verses to govern their lifestyle.

I shall endeavor within the context of this book to share with you wise counsel which will contribute in helping you cope successfully with any difficult situations you may be experiencing in your personal battles and rough situations in life. I also trust that you will be able to more clearly understand the blessing of all antagonistic experiences as a devoted Christian.

Bishop Eddie Jernagin

SPECIAL ACKNOWLEDGEMENT

When you are experiencing tough times, it's hard to believe that blessings are being unfolded. Yet God commands that those who love Him ought to give Him thanks for everything **(for all things work together for good to them that love God** – Romans 8:28), even tough times. Why – because He is there alongside of us, seeing us through them. **Didn't God promise He would never leave or forsake us!** (Hebrews 13:5)

Bishop Eddie Jernagin is one of the most powerful Christian writers this side of heaven. His handling of this subject, **"The Blessings of Tough Times,"** is simply amazing.

This is a must read for every Christian, especially those who think tough times are the enemy's playground. Looking at it from God's vantage point, tough times try our faith in Jesus and works our patience, thereby producing experiences that builds greater faith to fast-track us through future like or similar situations and circumstances. **It's a must read!**

Dr. Napoleon Rhodes

Prelate of The Convention of Covenanting Churches

INTRODUCTION

Why do bad things happen to good people? This is perhaps an age old question which has crossed the minds of many people. You have undoubtedly experienced many situations that have brought much pain and pressure in your life in spite of your devotion to God and your efforts to entreat others as you would have them entreat you.

Normally when we experience unjust treatment the usual **"why me"** question utters its inquisitive voice from within us. One's inability to answer that question often creates within one's inner self a feeling of anxiety and frustration. Much anxiety and anguish can stir within the frustrated individual when a bitter experience becomes magnified beyond the frustrated person's inability to see the possibility of any benefit to be gained from the testing experience.

Literally everything which transpires in life has a reason for being and does not stop because of certain bad situations. It is important, therefore, for each individual to discover positive means to deal with the bitter as well as the sweet without succumbing to the inevitable occurrence of tough situations.

An individuals allotted lifetime may consist of prolonged and painful defeats or a vast accumulation of wonderful victories. It depends in great measure upon one's choice of lifestyle and the choices that are made in aligning themselves with God's purpose and will as opposed to fallible philosophies of evil forces that war against the will of God for the mind of God's people.

Knowing the right thing to do when confronted by difficult situations can make the difference between abounding success as opposed to cataclysmic failure for following one's vain reasoning in the time of a tough crisis.

Following instincts of the flesh, in times of personal crisis, has taken a deadly toll upon humanity. Man needs a source stronger and wiser than himself if he is to endure hard times and challenging situations. He must reach beyond himself to discover the strength and Higher Wisdom he needs to successfully overcome opposing vices. He must acquire strategy from the Divine Source in handling tough situations – **there is no other source more knowledgeable!**

One might argue the point that there are ungodly people who never seek God's counsel and seem to excel through though experiences more successfully than many God fearing Christians. This may indeed be the case in some instances. However, looking at life from a temporal perspective and its temporal gain can never compare with eternal success and infinite redemption. **This unlimited blessing and hope is the destiny of those who choose to do things God's way!**

The Blessings

Of Tough Experiences

Overcoming Challenging Situations
To Eventual Success

By

Dr. Eddie Jernagin

CHAPTER 1

SHAKEN BUT NOT DEFEATED

September 11, 2001, a wonderful God-given picture-perfect day like thousands of blissful days gone by, except when the staggering news that confronted me and perhaps millions of other Americans as I awake from a comforting night of blissful slumber.

My routine inspirational practice of praise and thanksgiving to God flowed from my spirit as I awoke to greet the dawning of a typical sunny Southern California morning. The unwinding stretch and the usual yawn flowed through my person as I attempted to compose myself in preparation for the day's busy schedule that awaited my attention.

Reaching for the television remote, I pressed the power switch to catch up on the early morning news. I became intensely mesmerized as I observed speeding commercial aircraft crashing into the two towering landmark structures of the World Trade Center that dominated the blue skies of the mighty 'Bid Apple,' New York City.

Orange-colored flames of fire engulfed the caps of the two massive structures as emergency workers fought frantically to rescue thousands of office workers who occupied the two massive facilities. Then suddenly, without warning, in sequential order the mighty one hundred ten story twin towers plummeted to the earth as massive mushroom clouds of billowing smoke engulfed the sprawling skyscraper canyons as red hot columns of mighty steel beams plummeted in weakness to the earth's surface.

I saw hundreds of New Yorkers running frantically through the streets of the bustling metropolis as they desperately sought refuge from the danger and destruction of death that had already claimed thousands who had become unfortunate victims of this unprecedented historic calamity on American soil.

To the bewilderment of Americans, and the world population at large, it was revealed by the news media sources, that ungodly terrorists had spearheaded this evil plan of destruction upon society.

As appalling as these circumstances were, ironic acts of good began to surface, defying the evil that had been perpetrated upon humanity. Government officials began to pray, thousands who sought comfort and strength from God filled our churches. Patriotism began to surface, and American and foreign nations alike began to see a dire need for mutual alliance, understanding, compassion and brotherhood for all mankind, regardless of race, religion and other factions that exist to separate us. The freedoms we Americans so often seem to take for granted took on greater value when the principles of our freedom become threatened.

~ GOD CONSCIOUSNESS ~

It never ceases to amaze me how inherent good always seems to surface in times of evil imposition and death defying circumstances. Tough experiences have a way of making man more God conscious, especially when his back is against the wall and all other avenues of His trust have began crumbling in times of severe crisis.

America was shaken by this unprecedented act of cowardice inflicted upon her land, but the nation refused to be defeated which reveals her resiliency and determination to bear the burden. In the midst of the gross evil which transpired, the staggering occasion presented an ideal opportunity for this to be the churches' – and American's – finest hour to continue to seek God's strength in defiance of evil, and adhere indeed to the creed, **"In God we trust."**

If the attack which came upon America causes the nation to turn towards God for guidance, great will be the strength of the Nation! The following biblical passage expresses God's promise to his people: *"If my people, which are called by my name, shall humble themselves and pray, and seek my fact and turn from their wicked ways; then will I hear from heaven, and will forgive their sin, and will heal their land."* (2 Chronicles 7:14)

CHAPTER 2

WHY ME?

The **"why me"** syndrome has perhaps occurred countless times in the minds of individuals who have often wondered why a rough situation has occurred in their life. You have undoubtedly had your share of problems that were troublesome. Perhaps, as far as you are concerned, you've had more than enough! As puzzling as negative experiences can sometimes be, there are destined times when they must occur if we are to reach a certain level of maturity.

~ MATURITY ~

Have you ever witnessed a person of advanced age act in a fashion that did not parallel their age level? The unwise action of that individual brought to the surface a revelation of their immaturity.

Chronological age progression occurs when twelve months or three hundred and sixty-five days have elapsed. Maturation, however, does not necessarily follow that sequential order. Maturity is accomplished as we learn how to handle difficult situations without self-destructing, or learn how to utilize those experiences to strengthen our positive resolve.

For the Christian to mature in their walk with Christ, there are challenging moments of Divine design for the expressed purpose of elevating the child of God. When restraint is exercised instead of releasing your emotion to inflict punishment upon the offender, a positive level of

Christian maturity is brought to the surface to bring conviction upon the offender as to their wrong gesture towards you. The blessing in this case is exemplified when the Christian who has been offended is given the opportunity to do the right thing which in turns gives the offender the opportunity to observe the unique quality of Christian character first hand.

~ YOUR LIFE TESTIFIES ~

Many times an offender is brought under conviction by what his observes in the righteous character of a Christian. Whenever a Christian does what is right in reference to injustice, Christ becomes lifted up! It was Christ who said, *". . . if I be lifted up from the earth, will draw all men unto me."* (John 12:32)

Opportunity is always presenting situations for the children of God to allow their life to testify that the presence of Christ is at hand. Whenever a tough circumstance is prevalent, the residence of God's power within you is given an opportunity to prove its keeping ability to prevent you from falling! The stabilizing factor that is God's presence within you provides the peace you need in the midst of the raging storm, *"And the peace of God, which passeth all understanding, shall keep your hearts and minds through Christ Jesus."* (Philippians 4:17)

Any time the **"why me"** syndrome arises in the midst of your storm, always try to let God be glorified. You will undoubtedly always come out the winner! The glory of God is exemplified in your Christian demeanor when restraint and humility are exercised, when leaving the battle to God's ability in helping you to overcome the evil attack. It is by the display of your humility and restraint and by your eventual success over your adversary, that the enemy becomes confounded. The godly act of your demeanor confirms God's ability to confound your foe.

The Apostle Paul said that the Saints (Christians) *"are accounted as sheep for the slaughter."* Christianity is a suffering way because we are partakers of Christ's suffering who is our founder! As He suffered, we also encounter various sufferings because of our identification with Him. Nevertheless, through every suffering experience of God's chosen ones, we are *"more than conquerors."* The warring experience is a set up for Satan's destined defeat! So then, if this is true, one should not ask the questions, **"why me?"** One should know that God knows the beginning from the ending; and if your faith is unshakable, you win and to God's credit goes the glory!

~FIVE FOLD EXPLANATION ~

The following represents a five-fold summation in answer to the **"why me"** question in reference to God allowing the righteous to temporarily experience certain antagonistic experiences: (1) God takes the foolish things to confound the wise; (2) God takes the weak things to confound the mighty; (3) God takes the base things to humble the exalted; (4) God utilizes the despised things to humble the noble; (5) God utilizes powerless things to bring to defeat the things that are powerful. **(See *1 Corinthians 1:25-29*).** The wisdom of God's strategy is far beyond the finite comprehension of man!

Never allow the **"why me"** syndrome to dominate your thought pattern. Develop the attitude which says, **"To God be the glory."**

CHAPTER 3

LOVE, FAITH & OBEDIENCE

Irrational reasoning is often a catalyst for a lack of understanding the positive benefits inherent in testing experiences. Through varied experiences of opposing challenges and victories over such matters, the potential for irrational thought of the committed Christian is able to yield to the will of God knowing that, *"all things work together for good,"* as the scripture professes, *"to them that love God."* Love is willing to suffer wrong when a greater good is to be accomplished.

~ LOVE SUPERCEEDS PAIN ~

The key to endurance and eventual overcoming a trial is predicated upon your love for God, faith in His faithfulness, and obedience to His will. Love is the ultimate virtue that supersedes painful situations. A typical example is the suffering of Christ who endured the pain of crucifixion all for the love of humanity and for the will of God The Father! The pain he suffered brought healing to humanity and the gift of eternal life to whosoever will submit to the will of God.

~ LOVE TESTED ~

The ultimate test of love is the pain and suffering one is willing to endure for the sake of love's commitment to a noble cause regardless of the painful price! I am sure it was difficult at most for the patriarch Abraham to be willing to give his son, Isaac, whom he dearly loved, for a burnt sacrifice in response to God's request. The mental anguish of the astounding command would be more than most would be willing bear. However, Abraham's love and willingness to obey God, regardless of the difficulty, became his motivation to obey the Higher Power! Abraham's faith in God's sovereign will caused him to embrace the belief and vision that God was able to raise his son up after his obedience in doing God's will.

~ ABRAHAM'S TEST ~

Difficult moments bring out the best or worst that is within us. It causes us to be placed in a position of having to exercise faith to see beyond the confronting antagonism. Abraham was able to do just that when he was challenged to offer Isaac, his endeared son, as a sacrifice. His ability to embrace, by faith, the power and faithfulness of God to resurrect his son gave him the necessary strength to obey God's challenging demand.

The act of submission, exercised by Abraham, brought a reciprocal response from God to provide the substitutionary sacrifice of a ram. Faith, love, and loyal obedience are positive gestures that please the very heart of God when utilized to fulfill His Devine Will through every trying experience!

The believer's love for God must be stronger than the trying confrontation of suffering encountered for righteousness' sake. Genuine love is willing to suffer the wrong encountered because within the spiritual makeup of love is the unique willingness to forgive the unjust offense.

~ WHO SHALL SEPARATE US? ~

Paul asked a question in his epistle to the saints of Rome: *"Who shall separate us from the love of Christ?"* He gave a list of opposing examples such as, persecution, famine, distress, nakedness, peril or sword. Paul then answered his own question by saying none of these forces would be able to separate the devout believer from the love of God that operates in Christ Jesus!

~ LOVE UNSTOPPABLE ~

The **"Jesus kind of love"** working within the believer is stronger than death because it operates from a Divine perspective and nothing can stop it! It operates in the supernatural agape realm. Regardless of opposition directed towards it, this unique love manifests and maintains its attributes. It is love beyond measure. **"Trying experiences"** bring the positive power of love's manifestation to the surface that bewilders and defies evil schemes!

~ FAITH IS NECESSARY ~

In the Lord's faithfulness to deliver you in storm-filled moments, faith is essential if the warring battle is going to ultimately benefit you. Suffering for Christ's sake cannot be beneficial if faith, which Christ is the author and finisher, is not given an opportunity to prove its worth. The **"God kind of faith"** is at its best when attacked. David slew the giant Goliath with this kind of faith! The children of Israel walked across the Red Sea! Joshua prayed and stopped the progression of the sun! Jesus, the Chief Architect of our faith, overcame death, hell and the grave!

You discover the blessing and value of your faith in God when He helps you to overcome the so-called impossible situation. When you flow with the power of faith you always abound in and over tough situations.

~ GOD'S GLORY MANIFESTED ~

God does not always remove the tough situation, but He blesses you regardless of the situation. How many times have you prayed to God to remove a painful encounter and He didn't? Nevertheless, He made you a fire within the fire! Or you were able to dance the dance of joy within the storm! God has astounding ways of allowing His glory to manifest in the presence of difficult encounters while your faith in Him brings you out on top! Thank God for the **"God Kind of Faith."**

CHAPTER 4

OVERCOMING HURDLES

Becoming proficient at dealing with life requires overcoming many hurdles along life's journey to get where you want to go. A competent hurdler must master and develop his skills to become the best that he can be if he is to compete with others who are also competent at what they do in the same sports activity.

Hurdling is a racing sports activity that requires the competitors to overcome a row of difficult frame-lie barriers place across a racecourse to be leaped over by the contestants until they reach the finishing line, sometimes one hundred or more yards away.

Strength, speed, stamina, and proper technique are all necessary for a proficient hurdler to become a master of his sports specialty. Hard work, practice, proper diet, and persistency are required of the competitor if he is to be the best at what he does.

In many ways the Christian journey can be similar to that of a competitive hurdler. You as a Christian must be willing to pay the price of overcoming many hurdles if you are to gain the reward of heaven as your destined eternity. You must daily practice the morals of Christian principles being determined that you will be the best that you can be as a devoted Christian.

Paul, the Apostle, likened the Christian journey to a competitive race in Philippians 3:13-14. *"Brethren I count not myself to have apprehended: but this one thing I do forgetting those things which are behind, and reaching forth unto those things which are before. I press toward the mark for the prize of the high calling of God in Christ Jesus."*

Holy ambition and the desire to hear God say **"well done"** in response to Christian service is a noble desire. Obtaining the goal of holy living, however, demands overcoming the hurdles of evil devices to attain that goal. The press Paul alludes to in his Philippians' discourse implies confrontational resistance that you must conquer to obtain success. The blessing of your successful endurance reveals the worth of your spiritual resolve. A Christian's so-called resolve is worthless if he cannot endure the press. The worth and proof of your resolve surfaces when you have endured the storm and conquered life's hurdles.

Diligent practice of the Christian faith shines forth as an illuminating beacon for the entire world to see when you have conquered life's storm and defied **"demonic hurdles"** that tried to destroy your faith in the Christian pursuit of victory!

I am convinced there are certain devoted Christians selected by God to face certain bearers in life as an example of what it means to be a good Christian soldier who has weathered the storm.

~ IT'S A SET-UP ~

In the book of Job, Satan and God were conversing and God said to Satan, *"Hath thou considered my servant Job."* Little did Satan realize that he was walking directly into a sovereign set up God had planned for his defeat and the Lord's glory. Job was challenged to the very core of his life, yet he overcame the tough hurdles by maintaining his integrity. Job lost much in the battle but he won the war and gained more than he lost when he successfully overcame Satan's strategy!

~STAYING FOCUSED ~

I can imagine that when a competitive hurdler is crouched at the starting line to compete in an event, he experiences the gamut of emotions that crosses his mind. He must be able nevertheless, to throw all the negatives from his mind and accentuate the positive. He must be confident that he can win! He must focus on the positives and follow through on the fundamentals and plans he has practiced.

When the starter's gun goes off he must thrust himself toward the finishing line not looking back but straight ahead towards his goal. He must finish the race to win the prize.

In your pursuit of Christian perfection you must be as the hurdler and maintain your focus by following through on the defining principles you've read in God's Word and apply them in practice to your Christian devotion. You are in the race to win, not to be second or anything less! You are destined to win when steadfast biblical truth is your motivational source.

The celebration for winning is so sweet when you can look back once you have won and see the experiences you have conquered to gain so much more than you've had to endure. The sacrifice, toil, and pain, seems worth the price you've had to pay when you can enjoy in victory the rich rewards of all your efforts!

CHAPTER 5

IT'S NOT YOUR BATTLE

Have you ever by impulsive instinct taken upon yourself the task of retaliation to a confronting battle and later regretted your rash decision? If so, you are not alone! Much too often we are prone to exercise zeal that reflects wrong thinking and irrational decision making.

~ CARNAL IMPULSES ~

As a young understudy of Jesus, Peter was often guilty of making hasty actions. When the Roman soldiers came to take Christ into custody, as He prayed in the garden prior to his date with crucifixion, Peter was quick to react by taking his sword and cutting off the ear of one of the soldiers in defense of Jesus.

He did not realize that the battle was not his to fight, but it was God's opportunity to show his faithfulness in the time of the tough situation. Peter's carnal impulsiveness blinded his awareness of God's Divine providence for Jesus to experience that defining moment.

Christ forbade confronting strife with strife. He informed Peter that, *"They that take the sword shall perish with the sword." (Matthew 26:25)*.

Spiritual battles cannot be won by physical retaliation and carnal strategy. We must be aware of the fact that the **"battle is not ours."** As the scriptures inform us, *"The battle is the Lord's!"*

~SPIRITUAL ESSENCE ~

No weapon in God's arsenal, whether defensive or offensive, is of a carnal nature. Every weapon we read about in God's armor has a spiritual essence: (1) Truth, (2) Righteousness, (3) The Gospel, (4) Faith, (5) Salvation, (6) the Word of God, and (7) Prayer. *(Ephesians 6:11-18)* What an awesome arsenal!

The Christian must realize that every battle, where you as a Christian become the target, is not always a personal attack with you solely in mind. It's actually a battle against God. You are only the indirect object because of God's love for you and your devout stand you take for God in your love and commitment to His righteousness. Satan knows he cannot defeat God **"one on one,"** so he attacks that which belongs to God out of envy and defiance of God's rule and influence in their life.

Whenever a battle rages in your life, your relinquishing the pressure of the confrontation as you confide in the Lord's ability to be your defense places the warfare in His capable hands. When this is done, **"no weapon that is formed against you will prosper!"** You have the infallible assurance of the Word of God to back you up! *(See Isaiah 54:17)*

God knows how to handle the fight! He does not fear opposing confrontations. He uses them to demonstrate His prowess over them! It is the demon forces of hell that tremble when they hear the name of Jesus! God is a dominator! He consumes the adversary! *"For the Lord thy God is a consuming fire, even a jealous God! (Deuteronomy 4:24)*

God is so thorough in His ability to fight for you until all there is for you to do, while he is doing the fighting, is to trust Him and give Him praise. Jehoshaphat and his people did exactly that when outnumbered by their adversaries in the time of their crisis.

~ PRAISE TO VICTORY ~

Jehoshaphat was given instruction to confront their allied foe with the spiritual weapon of praise unto God's holiness. Their jubilant praise unto the Lord's holiness ushered them up into a fearless realm of spiritual strength and boldness to ultimate victory. When you are going through a battle against the enemy, praise and thanksgiving are vital to your frame of mind, and it helps to get you through the storm to eventual success!

Much too often we are prone to magnify the opposing situation allowing our praise to be held captive by what we see. If you can see the battle as not being yours to fight, but an opportunity for God's glory to be made manifest, you are a step ahead of your enemy which should bring out your best praise even before the war has ended!

Perhaps you cannot see the end of the struggle, but through praise you embrace the victory. Because you know that God never loses a battle, with this in mind you cannot **"call those things that are not as though they were"** because God is on your side, if you are in His will.

Spiritual battles in God's Divine providence are but steppingstones to greater glory for the Lord's honor and your spiritual enrichment and maturity. Knowing this before the battle begins should help to alleviate ignorance to the fact that the battle is not yours but God's and you are the benefactor of the whole experience!

CHAPTER 6

SPIRITUAL WARFARE

The following passage addresses our spiritual battle against evil. *"For we wrestle not against flesh and blood, but against principalities, against powers, against the rulers of Darkness of this world, against spiritual wickedness in high places."* (Ephesians 6:12)

~ SUBMISSION TO THE HOLY SPIRIT ~

The word **"wrestle"** in the preceding biblical text implies an intense conflicting struggle. An exertion of energy is necessary in any wrestling confrontation. From a logical perspective, the physically stronger subject in a wrestling contest will undoubtedly be the winner. However, from a spiritual perspective, physical prowess is not always the determining factor for victory. Since spiritual warfare is in the intangible realm, submission to the Holy Spirit is vital to winning spiritual war.

~ THE UNSEEN FORCE ~

As a minister of the gospel of Jesus Christ, my tenure of service has brought me into contact with thousands by way of revival campaigns, radio and television, and personal one-on-one counseling. It's evident to me as a result of being in the people business, that most of our human struggles have to do with contending with unseen oppositional forces and the difficulty we often experience in understanding spiritual conflicts we encounter.

Even though many of our confrontations are with other human beings, it's important to know that behind every human confrontational conflict, is the stimulus of unseen forces. Human conflicts are spiritually infused. Every action of the flesh is actually motivated by a spirit. Therefore, if we are to be successful in combating evil forces (spirits), we must learn how to fight evil spirits with the Holy Spirit. Our weapons of warfare must not be carnal, if we are to succeed!

When it comes to an unexpected attack from the enemy of righteousness, the element of surprise can often be overwhelming. Foreknowledge and spiritual preparation to counter this kind of attack is advantageous to the Christian's stability in handling the antagonistic situation. The Word of the Lord exhorts us not to think of it as a strange occurrence when these moments arise in the Christian experience. *(See 1 Peter 4:12-13)*

~ YOUR SURVIVAL KIT ~

Spiritual armor is necessary for proper defense in the spiritual battle encountered in spiritual warfare. Carnal means are not sufficient to gain victory in such an encounter. One's battle in the spirit requires spiritual strategy and spiritual combative knowledge based upon Higher Wisdom, which comes from the Mind of God who is our fortress!

Knowledge of scripture alerts the believer to future oncoming attacks of the enemy. Although his attacks are often sudden, the element of surprise should be understood in the context of the facts that are revealed in the Holy Scripture concerning the unseen battles that lurk to overtake you.

The Word of God Is an informative and defending source. Adherence to the Word's wise counsel is vital to victory over the ensuing conflict. The spiritual strategy inherent within its counsel never fails! (Again I purposely repeat this fact – it is extremely important to your spiritual survival.)

We are exhorted in the Scripture to *"put on the whole armor of God!"* Nothing in God's armor is of a carnal nature. His armor can be likened to a spiritual survival kit that consists of faith, salvation, the gospel, righteousness, truth, and prayer. *(Ephesians 6:14-18)*

~ PROOF ~

The strength and infallibility of God's Word is proven from Genesis to Revelation. Fires have been quenched, the dead have been raised, and raging waters have been commanded to cease their fury! I could go on and on, but earthly volumes cannot contain the wonders of the Word's power to conquer warring vices.

~ ULTIMATE TRUTH ~

God's Word can predict imminent victory in the face of apparent and visible defeat, because it's encompassed by the essence of God who sees and knows all! The Holy Scriptures declare that *"in the beginning was the Word, and the Word was God!"* Who but an awesome God can call those things that are not, as though they were? Entering into spiritual warfare without the sword of the Spirit (God's Word) is like going into battle without strong foundational preparation. Always trust the wise counsel of this Ultimate Truth – it will always bless you regardless of the tough experience.

The storm may not be over, but you can shout in the storm because the blessing is imminent if you're abiding in the Word and the Word is abiding within you! The blessing is inherent in the truth that makes you free!

CHAPTER 7

DEMONIC FACTIONS

The subject of demonology always seems to stir interest within the inquisitive mind. Jesus had many confrontations with evil spirits during the course of his ministry as He literally walked the earth. He managed nevertheless to defeat those imposing spirits by exercising faith and spiritual authority inherent within the anointing upon his life.

~ DEMONIC ORIGIN ~

Just as all human existence has its origin in God who is the Creator, demonic forces have their origin that originates in Satan. Satan, who is the author of confusion and evil, tries to compete with God for the being of God's human-creation.

When people refuse to submit to the Lord they become vulnerable to evil influence. When evil is permitted to rule the human spirit it thrives on the spiritual weakness and rebellion of humankind.

~ LUCIFER'S DISMISSAL ~

When Lucifer attempted to compete with God while inhabiting heaven, his rebellious confrontation led to his dismissal and demotion from an archangel of radiance to a fallen spirit of evil and disgrace. The dismissal of Satan from heaven gives to those who are called to be Saints the right to also cast satanic influences out of their affairs when evil devices attack them.

The Word of the Lord declares that we have been given authority over all the power of the devil. Jesus also declares that all power in heaven and earth is in his hands. We who are in Christ must realize that Satan has no legal authority to defeat us. He only usurps authority from those who give up their God-given gift of dominance in fear of his deceit.

When Adam and Eve acted contrary to the Creator's command not to eat of the forbidden tree, their disobedience adversely affected all of human creation. When you and I in our confrontations with evil and tough situations fail to utilize spiritual authority to overcome adverse forces, we live beneath our privilege as overcomers. Our actions to such confrontations should be that which God did when Satan rebelled in heaven. God cast him out! We must also cast Satan away through and by the power of the Holy Ghost that gives to us dominance over demonic evil.

When Jesus was confronted with Satan's challenge to jump from the pinnacle of the temple, Christ did not oblige Satan's evil scheme. He utilized the authority of **"Truth"** to overcome the evil scheme of entrapment. The devil can quote truth but he has no spiritual authority to make it work as a deceptive conquering device! The opposite is true, however, for Christians who are true followers and worshippers of Christ, the word Christ denotes **"the anointed one."** The true Saints of the Lord are filled with this anointing when we are baptized in the Holy Ghost! It's with this authority that we can use God's truth with authority to cast away evil.

It is inevitable that the opportunity will present itself for us to discover the inherent power we, as Christians, possess to allow this anointing to be manifested. Satanic forces are always presenting themselves to defy our devotion to God's will for our life. It's the anointing we possess, however, that always destroys the yoke when we exercise its availability to us in annihilating the work of demonic intrusiveness.

If demonic spirits are to survive they must have living beings to manifest themselves in. If the anointing is to do its effective work, it must have living vessels to exercise its manifestation. This is why God has anointed the church! When the church is flowing in the Holy Spirit, she is flowing in the anointing. Thus, the satanic kingdom is forever being torn down and it cannot survive when the church is flowing in the unity of the faith and the power of the anointing. The Bible states, *"The yoke shall be destroyed because of the anointing."*

~ IT'S IN THE WORD ~

I once invited a minister to the church I pastored to conduct three nights of teaching services. I never shall forget the night he was confronted with a woman demonically possessed. The late Dr. Floyd Miller was quite unemotional in his presentation of ministry. I had always been accustomed to seeing demonstrative emotions when observing the casting out of demons. On this occasion however, Dr. Miller relaxed, sat on the side of the platform and began quoting scripture to the demonic spirits. Amazing results followed. Demons were cast out, the woman was set free, and the Word of God prevailed! **Nothing is more effective in overcoming times of tough situations like the truth, which sets you free!**

God has equipped the church with an anointing that represents spiritual qualification authorizing the believer to use the ability of truth to overcome evil. The recent attack of antagonistic forces on September 11, 2001 in New York City was more than just an attack on the mortar, steel, and stone of the twin towers. I believe it was an attack on Christianity, which America predominately embraces.

Demonic factions have fought against God's will for man since Adam and Eve. They will attempt to do so until the new heaven and earth are finally established. The anointing, however, is one of the church's most valuable spiritual assets to combat such enemy intrusions.

CHAPTER 8

THE ANOINTING

The evils that are present on earth demand the need for an authority which counters and resist such forces. With this fact in mind, God has equipped His Spiritual Body, the church, with spiritual ability to combat these sources. This special endowment is known as **"the anointing."**

Each victory over every spiritual battle works as a conditioning process that leads to a greater anointing. The anointing is a representation of the Lord's presence and authority manifested in believers being used as reservoirs in conquering warring forces.

The anointing (Divine Energy) is at its best when confronting antagonistic situations. Opportunity is always presenting itself on a daily basis for this astounding spiritual authority to be utilized.

You may recall the occasion when Jesus and the disciples saw a blind man who was without sight from birth. The inquisitive disciples asked Jesus why was the man blind? Jesus replied that, *"it was for the works of God to be manifested."* (John 9:3)

I believe it was not so important to know why the physical impairment as it was to know the remedy to the prevailing problem! The blind man's condition presented a golden opportunity for the anointing in the Lord's life to destroy the yoke of blindness and bring glory to the power of the Lord's awesome dominance over so called **"tough situations."**

~ THE ANOINTING IS NECESSARY ~

It's vital for every believer to have the anointing upon their life. Great works cannot be performed when this spiritual authority is not resident in a professing believer. Yokes are destroyed when confronted by the awesome presents of this unique spiritual endowment.

One might challenge the point that the previous statement is not necessarily true because there are skilled physicians, proficient lawyers and great intellectual minds that perform many wonderful and amazing wonders without professing to be spiritual or religious. As noble as these professions may be, they cannot cure spiritual ills!

The anointing that operates within the life of the believer is capable of setting the total person free – mind, soul and body! This unique spiritual quality performs as God performs. It is directly reflective of His Divine Authority operating through earthly human vessels that have been commissioned by the Heavenly Father to continue the ministry of Christ in the earth. It is reflective of the Kingdom of God operating in the earthly realm.

~ THE KEYS ~

The anointing is more powerful than any earthly challenge. It operates in the spirit realm with heavenly approval. The following scripture is proof of this fact! *"And I will give unto thee the keys of the kingdom of heaven: and whatsoever thou shalt bind on earth shall be bound in heaven; and whatsoever thou shalt loose on earth shall be loosed in heaven."* (Matthew 16:19)

The anointing is not predicated upon exterior or intellectual influence. It is based upon the Person of the Holy Spirit and one's submissiveness of faith, commitment and dedication to one's Divine Call.

Although various conflicts are all around us, when the anointing that is resident within the believer is allowed to abound, the vice of confronting conflicts are destroyed as it confronts the prowess of the anointing. **This astounding endowment from the Lord has no equal!**

~ THE CHRIST ~

The name Christ means *"the anointed one."* Jesus, who is *"The Christ,"* was endowed with Super Natural abilities, which astounded multitudes! It was daily evident that this unique authority was resident in His life. The Bible declares that He, *"went about doing good, and healing all that were oppressed by the devil..."* (Acts 10:38) these opposing forces always brought out the best of what Jesus had to offer.

The anointing gravitates towards trouble! If you are anointed, you should not be running from difficult situations. You should be conquering them. You should not be fleeing from the enemy, rather you should be overcoming his evil strategy!

~ THE WILDERNESS EXPERIENCE ~

The Spirit of God led Jesus into the wilderness to be tested by opposition! This was necessary for the preparation for a greater works ministry. If Jesus had flunked the test in the wilderness when challenged by Satan, He could not have proclaimed with authority that, *"the spirit of the Lord is upon me, because he hath anointed me to preach the gospel to the poor, heal the brokenhearted, preach deliverance to the captives, recovering of sight to the blind," etc.* (Luke 4:18) these are opposing forces for which the anointing is authorized to destroy.

~ OLD & NEW COVENANT ANOINTING ~

Under the old covenant, this Super Natural quality was given to a selected few. In the New Testament, it was made available to the entire body of believers gathered in the upper room on the day of Pentecost. This unique authority was evident as the New Testament church became highly automated, going from house to house conquering strongholds of sin, sickness and disease! The New Testament church was perpetually seeking opportunities to exercise the spiritual authority of this unique gift.

~ UNKNOWN TONGUES ~

The initial introduction of unknown tongues (speaking in tongues) that was given to the New Testament church on the Day of Pentecost is often misunderstood by many today. When the manifestation of speaking in tongues is not accompanied by a demonstration of deliverance administered by today's church, which represents Christ who is **"The Anointed One,"** the intended purpose of the gift is not totally fulfilled! Speaking in unknown utterances is a sign that believers are filled with the Holy Spirit. It signifies that the anointing is prevalent in the believer's life. The proof of its dynamism is manifested whenever tough conditions are conquered as a result of the anointing being exercised by spirit-filled believers.

~ ANOINTED TO SERVICE ~

The believer must keep in mind that he / she is never given this Super Natural ability for self glorification. A gift of this magnitude is never to be hoarded. It is designed to show forth the works of the Kingdom of God, and testify of the fact that the Kingdom of Heaven is at hand for mankind to witness universally!

CHAPTER 9

COUNT IT ALL JOY

1 Peter 1: 6-7 states: *"So be glad! There is wonderful joy ahead, even though the going is rough for a while down here. These trials are only to test your faith, to see whether or not it is strong and to see whether or not it is strong and pure. It is being tested as fire test gold and purifies it – and your faith is far more precious to God than mere gold; so if your faith remains strong after being tried in the test tube of fiery trials, it will bring you much praise and glory and honor on the day of his return!"* 1

The One Year Bible (The Living Bible)

~ EXAMINATION ~

One of the most difficult things to do is rejoice when being tested. It is important to know that a test is designed as an evaluation of what is known by the one being tested. A lack of spiritual preparation for testing leads to failure. Putting on the armor of God equips you to take the test. The value of your spiritual armor cannot be personally known until it is tested.

I am not one who cherishes the thought of taking an exam. I remember quite vividly the time of my having to pass an exam to become a life insurance agent. My instructor assured the class that the examination would not be difficult if we studied for the multiple-choice test properly.

~ 3-D MEASURE ~

In preparation for the multiple-choice exam, we were given a practice examination revealing incorrect answers as well as the correct answers. When studying the sample exam the instructor told the students to focus on the correct answers and ignore the wrong choices. By so doing whenever we would take the real official test the right answers would automatically jump out at us because we did not focus on the wrong choices while we studied the practice exam. Sure enough, when I took the official examination that consisted of one hundred questions, I passed the exam with **"flying colors."** The right answers seemed to jump out in 3-D as I read each question!

When a Christian disciplines himself to study **"the Word"** he is given right answers for overcoming the test of life. In times of evil confrontation the right answers will stand out in 3-D measure if he has studied properly! This is a major contribution to **"counting it all joy"** when we are challenged. You will inevitably win when you practice biblical principles. No way can you lose when you dedicate yourself to its guidance! If I seem to be redundant of this fact, it's because it bares repeating!

~ JOY AND CONFIDENCE ~

Joy is inherent in knowing that you are going to win because you have the right answers. **One who knows the right answer and chooses by personal choice the wrong one should not complain when he is defeated.** Jesus endured the death of the cross because He chose the will of the Father, and He endured the pain because of the *"joy that was set before Him!"* He knew that He would overcome regardless of the tough situation.

~ DESTINED TO WIN ~

Committed Christians are eternally destined to win. They may be persecuted, misunderstood, falsely accused, misused and abused! Through Christ, however, they are destined to win regardless of how it appears during the agony of suffering. The Saints' ability to envision by faith their destined success should erupt into a crescendo of joy as they envision by faith that the best is yet to come!

James' exhortation to *"count it all joy"* came at a time when Jewish Christians were scattered in many geographical locations because of persecution. James realized, however, the importance of having supernatural joy regardless of the odds. He knew that tough times contributed to the growth of patience, the development of character, and preparation for dealing with future tough situations. The contribution of all this has contributed mightily to the posterity of Israel as a strong nation even in these contemporary times.

~ JOY IS A DEFENSE ~

Spiritual joy confuses Satan's strategy and bewilders his psyche. When you are smiling instead of frowning, when you are happy instead of being sad, *"down and out,"* it woks against the enemy's strategy. But when you allow these negatives to rule your spirit, you play into Satan's hands. He thrives off your misery when joy is not present within you. When joy is present within you, it helps to defend you from the attack. It gives you an upper hand when it is utilized as an important spiritual arsenal in your day to day battles with the evils of the world's unfair systems of unequal justice!

CHAPTER 10

PUT ON YOUR BEST FACE

There's nothing more self-defeating than to be going through a tough encounter with an adversary and allowing your foe to see you physically and emotionally at your worst! This kind of projected image increases the confidence of your enemy and fortifies his psychological ploy to intimidate and defeat you.

Please know that Satan is not all knowing! Only God Almighty is omnipotent (unlimited power), and omniscient (knowing all things). Satan only usurps authority as weak-minded individuals relinquish their dominance. The act of usurpation is always encouraging to the offender when you allow him to bully or usurp your God given authority to be the dominator.

Although it may not be always easy to do, it's important for you to maintain a positive image of power in your appearance and mental state though you may be trembling from within. You should never give the enemy a clue of any weakness you may have. Speak audibly or silently to your negative emotions with authority and allow your strong image to be projected. It will work wonders in your strategy of combat against the enemy! You must try never to let your own fear defeat you. It can often be your worst enemy.

~ PSYCHOLOGICAL WARFARE ~

Many battles initiated by the enemy are a psychological ploy to defeat you in your mind. Psychological warfare can

47

often be more damaging than physical combat. In fact, your physical stability is enhanced by your mental strength. The Philistine giant, Goliath, was bigger in stature than little David, the ruddy shepherd boy. But David refused to be intimidated by the giant's size. The God that he served, the Lord God of Israel, spiritually infused him with boldness. David thus won the psychological war as well as the physical battle! He did not allow the giant's armor of physical stature to cause him to retreat from the challenge. He won the battle! (See *1 Samuel 17:45-48*)

~ NEVER NEGLECT YOUR APPEARANCE

Have you ever seen someone or been guilty yourself of not eating, combing your hair, bathing, or neglected your appearance or hygiene because of going through a tough experience? I have actually witnessed individuals who totally **"let themselves go"** because they were involved in an intense emotional encounter. I've often wondered why should anyone inflict such punishment upon himself when the enemy is already inflicting hurt and pain!

When you are going through a **"rough place"** put on your best face! Dress up, put on your best perfume or cologne! Sing a happy song! Pray a positive prayer! It's only a matter of time if you stay positive before the storm will pass! Psyche yourself up spiritually – it works wonders!

Having a **"pity party"** is self-defeating. It robs you of faith and joy that is necessary to your survival. These two spiritual elements also help to enhance your appearance. It makes it difficult for the enemy to detect any weakness that may be present within you! You should always take advantage of the positive assets of spiritual tools to enhance your image when you are at war against the enemy of righteousness! Remember, "put on your best face!"

"Pray when things go wrong,

Faith will keep you ever strong,

There's no need to be alarmed,

The Lord will take you in His arms!

Smile, trust and obey,

It matters not what the people say,

You are free from hurt or harm,

When Jesus takes you in His arms!"

"Put On Your Best Face"

CHAPTER 11

ROOTS WITH SPIRITUAL RESOLVE

The word **"resolve"** intimates various implications. In the context of keeping in oneness with our subject matter, I shall utilize the word **"resolve"** to denote a firm commitment in faithful determination of one's walk with God regardless of the cost or opposing circumstances.

Reflecting upon my childhood days, I remember very well an old song the Saints would sing during the high jubilant praise and worship services. The Spirit filled lyrics were as follows:

"He's sweet I know, He's sweet I know,

Storm clouds may rise, stormy winds may blow,

I'll tell the world, wherever I may go,

I have found the Savior, He's sweet I know.

I'm going through, I'm going through,

I'll pay the price whatever others do,

I'll take the way of the Lord's despised few

I started with Jesus, and I'm going through!"

~ TAKING A STAND ~

The preceding song expressed the strong resolve the Saints of old possessed in tough days of gross discrimination, long days of labor in the cotton fields, and days of meager financial possessions. Through the jovial singing of that old song and joyous dancing in the Spirit, they endured tough situations! We do well to be encouraged from the legacy they have left us!

~ SPIRITUAL ROOTS ~

It's a fact that the deeper the roots of plant life, the stronger the plant will be as it matures. Looking at this fact from a spiritual perspective in the life of a committed Saint of God, the same premise is true. Tough situations that are mastered causes the strength of your righteous resolve to take deeper root. Spiritual strength and growth becomes enhanced as trouble is victoriously overcome. Each success should enhance the strength of your spiritual roots of experience and positively add strength to your resolve.

~ PAUL TAKES A STAND ~

Apostle Paul's thorn in the flesh spoken of in *2nd Corinthians* chapter three is a clear example of the pain experienced by his being buffeted and the paradox of strength gained as a result of the antagonizing warfare. He was buffeted in mind as well as in body but he was strong in the Lord whose strength is never weak!

Paul's personal discovery of God's sustaining grace in his weakness contributed to his resolve to maintain strong faith during the conflict of warring situations. This in return gave added spiritual dimension to Paul's effective ministry.

If God had indeed granted Paul instantaneous physical relief in response to his urgent request for quick relief, the valuable revelation of the Lord's grace in the midst of his tough testing would have remained concealed. When Paul resolved to allow the Master's grace to manifest to his spiritual gain he was able to bask in the Savior's abounding measure or favor. He was also able to boast that *"most gladly therefore will I rather glory in my infirmities, that the power of Christ may rest upon me."* (2 Corinthians 12:9)

~ CHARACTER DEVELOPMENT ~

During the conflict of buffeting for the righteous ones, character development is God's divine providence in allowing such to transpire, therefore, the objective is noble. While going through this challenging process you must not allow yourself to develop a defeatist attitude. You should instead permit your **"spiritual roots"** to embrace God's favor. This kind of tough experience should not stop a devoted Christian from serving God. It should cause him to rely upon the Lord's sustaining grace to get him through the challenging process! You can never realize the sustaining sufficiency of the Savior's grace until you resolve to be steadfast in firm commitment to your spiritual calling. When the **"roots"** of your faithfulness becomes deeply implanted within God's assurance of grace, you become a well-established individual in character, patience, and devotion to your positive purpose in life!

~ DEVOTED PIONEER ~

As we are privileged to read about the patriarchs, prophets, and committed Christians of the past, it's important that Christian contemporaries continue to hold the banner high! Reaffirm the Christian faith by resolving to let nothing separate us from the love of our Lord!

God in His wise providence permits various experiences of life, as taxing as they may sometimes be, to buffet us. In the experience of the buffeting, the Word of God to which we have had exposure, has an opportunity to prove its worth in our life when we resolve to use it as a weapon. We'll discover the worth of its ability to sustain us.

CHAPTER 12

DIVINE PROVIDENCE

Adversity introduces a person to the reality of their real self. You are not the total of your real self void of suffering and temptation. The totality of who you really are as a person surfaces when bitter and difficult experiences are allowed to manifest themselves in your life. What you do and the way you react to various experiences reflects the summation of your overall person.

If you give up or throw in the towel because of antagonistic confrontations, your positive traits are diminished. The opposite is true however, when you are able to **"weather the storm"** and come out stronger because of the storm!

Divine providence is often difficult to comprehend when injustice seems to prevail. The divine wisdom of the Lord may sometimes lead to the **"Red Sea"** with the enemy on your trail. However, the Lord's divine providence will always lead to victory if you are willing to follow his leading.

~ THE JOSEPH SCENARIO ~

Joseph was betrayed and sold into foreign hands as a result of the jealousy of his own brothers towards him. As divine providence would have it, however while in exile, Joseph gained favor with his foreign neighbors and was elevated to the position of governor of Egypt! God's divine providence was at work in the entire scenario of events that transpired in Joseph's life. His favor with God and his foreign superiors placed him in a position of leadership that led to the rescue of those same brothers who were dying of starvation because of a severe famine which had griped the land (Read *Genesis 37-50)*

~ WHERE IS GOD ~

Have you ever wondered where God is when you are going through a tough situation? The truth of the matter is, He is in the same place that He was when His only son, Jesus was being crucified. He was there with Christ allowing His divine providence to take its course. The end result of the whole painful process came to positive fruition in the final analysis! Christ became the Redeemer of all human kind as a result of the pain that He suffered, and this act gave man a second chance at life. What Christ bore on the cross brought to fruition the prophetic uniqueness of His being and the realization of His messianic ordination!

~THE TRANSGRESSOR ~

One might be prone to wonder, as a result of reading this book, if it is divine providence for life to be that of abounding pain and struggle. To the trend of thinking, I must reply with a resounding – No! Ultimately living is designed to be one of overcoming the ensnarement of evil that is utilized by evil forces to defeat abundant living that is inherent in Christ Jesus. The Word of God says, *"The way of the transgressor is hard."* An individual who is prone to do things their own way will find life to be difficult. The transgressor's life is carnally motivated and usually ends in disaster unless repentance before God is offered. When you **"kick against the prick"** (God's will), you make your own way difficult.

Tough situations by divine providence will always lead to a revelation of God's power within you if you allow His will to take its course to accomplish the conquest of oppositional situations. We are created by the Supreme to be eternal creatures with unequaled authority to rule the earth!

The following passages from the book of Revelation reveal a profound picture of believers who overcome the world's system of sin, injustice, and tough situations:

"... It is done. I am the Alpha and the Omega, the Beginning and the End. To him who is thirsty I will give to drink without cost from the spring of the water of life. He who overcomes will inherit all this, and I will be his God and he will be my son. But the cowardly, the unbelieving, the vile, the murderers, the sexually immoral, those who practice magic arts, the idolaters and all the liars their place will be in the fiery lake of burning sulfur. This is the second death." *(Revelation 21:7-9)*

CHAPTER 13

AMAZING GRACE

One should always remember that so-called **"tough experiences"** are only so in the eyes of man, but never difficult for God! When looking at challenging experiences from the Lord's perspective they are only steppingstones to spiritual elevation!

Mounting experiences that have been conquered enriches the faith of the overcoming Christian. It enhances knowledge that creates spiritual insight into the importance of the power of worship and allegiance to the Lord. Also, it penetrates and defies the concealed strategy of Satan's deceptive motives.

~ CALM UNDER PRESSURE ~

I once heard an anointed servant of the Lord say that, **"the more antagonistic pressure that he is confronted with, the calmer he gets."** The premise for this trend of thought is that mounting victories over past experiences reveal that **"tough times don't last, tough people do!"** Past successes breed confidence that produces relaxation which in the heat of the storm. When this particular posture is taken, it's an indication of God's grace at work in the whole experience.

~ SUFFICIENCY OF GRACE ~

There are various times when a spirit of vexation tries to impose itself upon the mind with nagging confrontations. Be reminded, however, of what Jesus said to Paul in his time of being buffeted, *"My grace is sufficient for thee: for my strength is made perfect in weakness."* *(2 Corinthians 12:9)*

~ THE STRENGTH OF GRACE ~

There is an astounding strength factor that operates within the grace of the Lord when a child of God is going through a tough trail. It is the Savior's grace that provides the strength that is needed to endure affliction. Problems that you otherwise could not endure become bearable when God's amazing grace is working on your behalf.

When you are covered by grace you are elevated to a supernatural level that gives you a supernatural advantage over your foe! This is an important reason why we must be sensitive to the Spirit's direction when we are involved in battle. We must allow the supernatural strategy of the Supreme Spirit to direct our course. Grace that operates from the Spirit of the Lord bewilders your enemies' understanding to such an extent that they must eventually see how difficult it is to **"kick again the prick."** God has a way of confounding the enemy to such an extent that the enemy has to confess, *"Surely this must be the Son of God!"*

Having knowledge of the Master's grace, which is available to sustain you, gives you a tremendous advantage over adverse situations. You are always a step ahead when grace is there to back you up. Therefore, If in your battles of life you are always loosing it could simply be an indication that you are not permitting God's grace to complete its perfect work.

~ LOVE AND GRACE CONQUERS ~

Grace is a product that has its origin in God's love. Many times to the carnal way of thinking love is not the way to fight one's adversary. We have but to look to Jesus, however, for an example of what grace and love did for humanity. Through His love and grace we have been redeemed from the grips of death brought on by sin that is our enemy. *John 3:16* states, *"For God so loved the world, that He gave His only begotten Son, that whosoever believeth in Him should not perish, but have everlasting life."* What an act of incomparable grace!

If this act of love and grace can overcome sin, which is our enemy, should not this same grace be able to overtake our enemy when it is operational within us as believers and followers of Jesus Christ? We are His disciples and His grace lives within our being! His grace is at work in us bringing conviction upon our enemy so that, *"If God is for us who can be against us?"* So, don't fight us, join us!

Saul of Tarsus, the enemy of the Christian world, discovered this astounding grace on the way to Damascus to persecute the Saints. But when he came in contact with the Divine Power that was mightier than he, the love and grace of the Lord won him over! (See *Acts chapter 9)* Ironically, Saul, whose name was later changed to Paul after his Christian conversion, became one of the greatest apostles of all times with the exception of Jesus Christ!

May we who are committed believers and followers of Christ consider that we were once enemies to Christ because of our un-repented sins. But when we submitted to His will, grace and love we now have victory over sin!

The following old hymn should remind Christians of the ability of grace and its power to win when we allow it to bring conviction:

"Amazing grace! How sweet the sound,

that saved a wretch like me!

I once was lost, but now am found,

was blind but now I see.

'Twas grace that taught my heart to fear,

and grace my fears relieved;

How precious did that grace appear

the hour I first believed."

By John Newton

Grace befuddles the intellect of the offender. It conquers the emotion of fear. It defies the heat of fire, lock the jaws of lions, and overcomes the tempestuous storms at sea! The mystery of the power of grace that is concealed from the evil oppressor works as a potent defense for the elect of God. God Almighty who is the Supreme One employs it!

CHAPTER 14

DESTINY HAS PAINFUL MOMENTS

Destiny is an inevitable fact associated with life. Between life and death, both physical and spiritual pain is a reality of events that human life encounters.

Positive destiny has its moments of trouble and pain. The revelation of your positive destiny is predicated upon your ability to survive the pain and various antagonistic experiences that are necessary to reveal your destiny's true value. For an example, if your successful ending is to be a glorious beginning of reigning with the Lord throughout eternity, you must be willing to go through whatever it takes to reach and enjoy the supreme value of eternal life. Once you have reached the state of your eternal being, you will be able to reflect retrospectively on all you had to go through realizing the valuable lessons you learned along the way from all of life's **"trying situations"** you had to endure to obtain the incomparable gift of eternal life!

Obtaining spiritual maturity and eternal glory requires the endurance of things that causes the Christian to exercise godly character in the midst of painful situations. Overcoming such testing devices brings honor and distinction to the believer's association with Christ. Your expected end is much more enjoyable and glorious than the things you must go through to get there! When satanic evil aspires to stop, destiny says, **"don't give in!"** Your expected end is not eternal death that comes as a result of yielding to satanic ensnarements, rather your expected end is eternal life. It does not matter what others may think or say because of what you must endure. It's what God thinks that should be most important in your life. Destiny is calling you to an excepted end from God's perspective. What you have to suffer to get there is only temporary...! "In His (God's) favor is life: *'weeping may endure for a night, but joy cometh in the morning!'"* (Psalms 30:5)

For seventy oppressing years the Israelites were held in captivity to their Babylonian enslavers. The captivity was not intended to be their demise, from the Lord's perspective, but rather a designated period of time ultimately leading to a victorious expected end. Following is an overview of this historical scenario: *"The truth is this: you will be in Babylon for seventy years. But then I will come and do for you all the good things I have promised, and bring you home again. For I know the plans I have for you, says the Lord. They are plans for good and not for evil, to give you a future and a hope. In those days when you pray, I will listen. You will find me when you seek me, if you look for me in earnest."* (Jeremiah 29:10-14)

God's chosen people (Israel) made such a shambles of life by pursuing after pagan gods and heathenish ideologies. But whenever they would genuinely repent, their destiny was turned towards the embrace of God the Father who is everlasting love!

You also can have the privilege of access to God's marvelous love! Forever living in the compassionate arms of God that is destined to be your expected end, which ultimately leads to a glorious new beginning, void of any more **"tough experiences!"**

~ OVERCOMER'S DELIGHT ~

"Then one of the elders asked me, These in white robes where did they come from? I answered, Do, you know. And he said, These are they who have come out of the great tribulation; they have washed their robes and made them white in the blood of the Lamb. Therefore, they are before the throne of God and serve him day and night in his temple; and he who sits on the throne will spread his tent over them. Never again will they hunger; never again will they thirst. The sun shall not beat upon them, nor any scorching heat. For the Lamb at the center of the throne will be their shepherd; he will lead them to springs of living water and God will wipe away every tear from these eyes." (Revelation 7:13-17, 2nd NIV)

DAILY PRAYER PETITIONS

Lord God I thank you for the all powerful name of Jesus Christ! It is in His name that I offer up all of my Prayer petitions! I thank you that none will return void!

******

Father God I decree in the powerful name of Jesus Christ that sinful souls from the north, south, east, and west will come running crying what must I do to be saved!? Give me the wisdom and words of life to oblige their important inquisition!

******

Lord I thank you that all my repented sins are forgiven eternally and will never be used again to entangle me to eternal damnation!

******

I Confess upon your Word Lord that all my needs are met according to your riches in glory! I also confess upon your Word that, no weapon that is formed against me will prosper; and that every tongue that shall rise against me in judgment you will condemn! Thank you Lord!

******

■■■

I confess upon your Word Lord that all my needs are met according to your riches in Glory! I also confess upon your Word that no weapon that is formed against me will ever prosper!

******

Dear God in the name of Jesus Christ of Nazareth, my soul say's an eternal yes to your directions for my life! I trust your Divine judgment and ability to see what I can't see, and to know the things beyond my carnal understanding!

******

Father God in the name of Jesus Christ into your hands I commend my spirit, my faith, and my whole being to your will and glory!

******

Father God in the name of Jesus I pray that wherever life's journey may take me that I will always influence my space in a way that will point others to you, and to you go all the glory and honor that I may receive from others!

******

Dear God, I pray for the church at large, that we will indeed become as "one" in Christ even as you and your beloved Son Jesus are inseparably one!

******

Father God in the name of Jesus, I sanctify my mind unto your righteousness that I may be free indeed from everything that is not like you!

Lord, order my steps on a daily basis. May I possess an obedient spirit to pursue the cause that is ordained for me by you on a daily basis!

******

Father God in the name of Jesus look upon my dear mother in her senior years. Strengthen her on a daily bases. Thank you for giving her to me and for her leading me to accept Jesus Christ as my Lord and Savior!

******

Father God I thank you for being created within your image. I pray that I will always live up to this reality by the things I both do and say!

******

Lord God I thank you for the wonderful gift of life that you have made possible through Christ who is the ultimate answer to the human need!

******

Father God I decree that all of my family will be "Spiritually Born Again" and that we walk in love and oneness always putting you first in our lives!

******

I degree in Jesus name that I will walk in Gods Divine prosperity daily and influence my space in a positive way that others may see Christ in me and be drawn to him as I allow his light to shine within me!

■■

APPENDIX: "THOUGHTS TO PONDER"

◊ Adversity is an ever present foe in the adventure of life, but victory is the ultimate assurance to those who love God regardless of the situation

◊ The end of life's battles that have been conquered is only the beginning of eternal bliss to those who have endured the storms of life.

◊ Knowledge is valuable! Wisdom to apply knowledge helps to obtain eventual victory!

◊ "And ye shall know the truth and the truth shall make you free." John 9:32

◊ Observe the testings of life and study how to overcome them by using as your source of reference God's Word!

◊ If you study to know truth when the test comes, the truth will "jump out at you." Grab it! Apply it!

◊ Battles won prepare you with confidence to fight greater battles ahead!

◊ Passing your test promotes you to your next dimension in life. Each test you pass propels you closer to perfection!

◊ Faith plus Calvary equals your deliverance!

◊ A test is an evaluation of what you know. Life's testing can have a twofold affect on one's life: it either brings out the best or worst in you!

◊ God can see the good that the present rough experience will produce in your life towards the success of your bright future!

◊ The servant of the Lord always has a brighter day to look forward to no matter how dark it may seem in the present!

◊ The more staggering the odds, the more sweeter and astounding is the victory once the odds are overcome!

◊ God will allow the odds to prevail as a set up for Satan's eventual defeat!

◊ Your faith in God's ability to handle your situation will help to keep you calm in the mist of the storm.

~ NOTES ~

ABOUT THE AUTHOR

At the age of eighteen, Eddie Jernagin accepted the Divine Call to minister and over the many years his powerful and practical words have been a blessing to countless thousands.

For 37 years, Dr. Eddie Jernagin pastored the Christ Is The Answer Church in Los Angeles, California. He is a noted Conference Speaker, Counselor, Bible Teacher, Adviser, International Radio Personality, Author and Bishop.

In 2012, he founded and is the president of **"New Dimensions International Ministries."** It's the evangelistic Bible Preaching and Teaching Ministry of Dr. Jernagin that's taking the Gospel of Jesus Christ unto the whole world.

Dr.. Eddie Jernagin is a gifted writer of practical truth endeavoring to share vivid insights about life from a biblical perspective. He aspires to show how utilizing biblical principles as a guideline can provide righteous solutions for human kind to ultimately succeed beyond all negative obstacles.

Dr. Eddie Jernagin also serves as the Vice Prelate of the Governing Board and the Bishop of the Fourth Jurisdiction of The Convention Of Covenanting Churches.

His messages will inspire you to search the scriptures, study the Kingdom Principles of God, mature in your faith, listen and obey The Holy Spirit and walk in the victorious life that Christ has given you.

AVAILABLE MATERIALS BY BISHOP EDDIE JERNAGIN

Books:

Man's Inheritance

An eye-opening paraphrase of man's spiritual and physical acquisitions in history as a result of God's gift to His human creation. Bishop Jernagin expounds on man's origin and fall and concludes with man's eternal destiny.

Fulfilling Your Purpose

This book is written and produced to be used as an informative teaching manual. Space has been provided through the entire book so that your personal notes and comments can be written adjacent to each page of the book.

In this informative written work, Bishop Jernagin underscores reasons why some utilize their God-given potential to excel and why some fail. The writer intermingles positive information on how all can reach their God-given purpose to succeed in spite of past defeats.

Lessons For Life

Navigating the course for victorious living.

Communicating With God

A practical handbook on prayer revealing insight into developing a personal, effective communion with God, thereby leading to a wholesome life of abundance.

Exhortation On Faith

A practical handbook emphasizing the daily importance of walking with God by faith to obtain strength and wisdom in overcoming daily challenging confrontations to eventual success.

Opening The Door To A New Millennium

(A comprehensive approach to Christian Education).

This informative Seminar Syllabus by Bishop Jernagin reveals constructive suggestions on the church school. He says the **"church school"** concept will play an ever increasing role in the 21st century.

He further writes, **"secular education in today's society will not suffice to teach high moralistic living standards in the new millennium."** Dr. Jernagin shares positive insights on how to educate local churches in meeting the **"whole need of the whole person."**

Tracts or Pamphlets:

Faith In The Cross

Determination

Walking With Christ As Little Children

Welcome To The Sheepfold

How To Be Born Of The Spirit

MINISTRY CONTACT INFORMATION

Dr. Eddie Jernagin

New Dimensions Outreach Ministries

PO Box 976

Muncie, IN 47308

Telephone:

765-729-3648

Email Address:

bishopeddiej@aol.com

Website Address:

eddiejernagin.com

www.ingramcontent.com/pod-product-compliance
Lightning Source LLC
Chambersburg PA
CBHW062020040426
42447CB00010B/2086